Marvin Richardson Vincent

The Lord of War and of Righteousness

A thanksgiving sermon preached in the First Presbyterian Church, Troy,

N.Y., Nov. 24, 1864

Marvin Richardson Vincent

The Lord of War and of Righteousness
A thanksgiving sermon preached in the First Presbyterian Church, Troy, N.Y., Nov. 24, 1864

ISBN/EAN: 9783337085247

Printed in Europe, USA, Canada, Australia, Japan

Cover: Foto ©Lupo / pixelio.de

More available books at **www.hansebooks.com**

The Lord of War and of Righteousness:

A

THANKSGIVING SERMON,

PREACHED IN THE

FIRST PRESBYTERIAN CHURCH,

TROY, N. Y., NOV. 24, 1864.

BY

REV. MARVIN R. VINCENT,

PASTOR.

TROY, N. Y.:
A. W. SCRIBNER, PRINTER, CANNON PLACE.
1864.

TROY, *November* 25th, 1864.

Rev. MARVIN R. VINCENT,

    Dear Sir :

        The undersigned having listened with more than ordinary pleasure and satisfaction to your discourse delivered on the occasion of the National Thanksgiving on the 24th instant, and feeling desirous that the sentiments so ably and eloquently expressed by you should be more widely disseminated, would respectfully and earnestly request a copy of it for publication.

CHAS. A. HOLMES,	JOHN E. WOOL,
S. B. SAXTON,	JNO. EDWARDS,
HARVEY J. KING,	GILES B. KELLOGG,
E. C. WILLIAMS,	CHARLES P. HARTT,
GEO. T. BALCH, U. S. A.,	DAVID COWEE,
JOHN A. MILLARD,	MARTIN I. TOWNSEND,
JAS. H. HOWE,	JOHN SHERRY,
S. K. STOW,	WM. S. SEARL

C. S. HUBBELL.

TROY, *November* 26th, 1864.

Maj.-Gen. JOHN E. WOOL, Messrs. EDWARDS,

        HOLMES, KELLOGG, and others.

GENTLEMEN :

        In compliance with your request I herewith transmit to you the manuscript of my discourse of the 24th inst.

    Truly yours,

        MARVIN R. VINCENT.

SERMON.

Rev. xix, 11 : "And I saw Heaven opened, and behold a white horse; and he that sat upon him was called Faithful and True, and in righteousness he doth judge and make war."

The year, in its round, has brought us again to the traditional season for thanksgiving and prayer. In obedience to the call of our chief magistrate, we assemble, to make the first act of the day not one of festivity but of worship. But, however numerous our private grounds of gratitude, we are not to forget that the Thanksgiving-day is a national institution, and that the call to our present duty issues from the heads of government. It is but proper, therefore, that, whatever our private devotions may include, our public acts should be, as far as possible, unselfish; that each should merge himself in the great body politic, and bring to the public festival that offering in which we are *jointly* represented.

It would be natural to attempt to sum up, at this time, all the grounds for public thanksgiving; but such an attempt might well appal a wiser than myself. So vast is the field, so thickly crowded with the golden sheaves of Divine blessing, that the time would fail to harvest the whole, even if the mind did not become bewildered in the task. It is, therefore, better for us to select some one of the numerous lines of thought radiating from the occasion, and to pursue that, than to attempt to glean at random from all quarters of the field. And here, again, we are met by a custom that has acquired almost the sanctity of law. This day has been for years past, and especially since the breaking out of the present rebellion, set apart for the discussion of great political questions and issues. Yet, for myself, I must confess that late events and excitements have brought to my mind, if you will allow the expression, a *surfeit* of politics. I turn with relief from the contesting claims of candidates and the comparison of platforms. I shall not impeach my patriotism by this confession. I think that most, if not all of you, share the feeling with me. And now that the great event, fraught with so much apprehension and excitement, has quietly passed; now that the will of the people has been expressed, and, as I rejoice to believe, loyally acquiesced in by both parties, I have little inclination to fight the battle over, while I am yet far from admitting that the result has rendered farther discussion unnecessary, or that the time has even come for the pulpit to be silent. Much still remains to be done; much to be decided; much to be canvassed in the spirit of the highest christian statesmanship.

In reviewing the causes for thanksgiving, as they appear amid the ghastly horrors of war, one cannot fail to be struck with the peculiar relations which the present crisis has developed between war and christianity. Strange as is the fact, these two essentially opposite elements have been associated with an intimacy which has had no parallel in the history of the world, and which is adapted to call out the liveliest emotions of surprise and gratitude. To show, therefore, that these relations do not clash with our highest conceptions of christianity; that, in the order of God's providence, the two, while essentially opposed, may yet work harmoniously toward a common end; that even out of war may lawfully arise the materials for a sincere christian thanksgiving, and that He who rides upon the white horse is Lord both of war and of righteousness, shall be my task to-day.

The intimacy of these two relations grows, in no direct sense, out of the religious character of the conflict. The present war, though springing directly from a great national sin, was not a crusade against that sin. Religion did not enter as a direct and avowed element of the conflict. It had its share in heightening patriotism, in urging to duty, in confirming resolution in individuals; but the nation, as a nation, went into the war as a political necessity, in self defence, as a means of saving itself from political ruin. Out of a war like that to which the preaching of Peter summoned the fanatical rabble of Europe, a class of sentiments and results arose which, for distinction's sake, may be called religious. But the fact that distinguishes the present conflict from all others in history is, that out of a war undertaken solely on political grounds, with a tendency on the part of a large class to confine its explanation and settlement entirely to political grounds, and to resist all attempts to raise the questions of the day into the realm of morals; out of a war which is itself the result of as foul a sin as ever blackened history; out of a war which involved, as it proved, division on the most vital questions among those between whom union was a necessity of existence; out of a war which, more than any other, has aroused the worst passions of men, and signalized itself by the most fearful atrocities,—out of all this, God has developed a national humiliation, a disposition to press the issues of the hour to their moral bearings in

spite of opposition; a spirit of prayer and thanksgiving; a substitution of principles for men and
parties; a series of christian activities, christian
sympathies, christian charities, and an evangelical spirit of religious awakening and revival
which have never, in the world's history, marked
the progress of war.

It is an interesting, and perhaps necessary question just here, whether these results are solely
the creation of the war as a Divine instrument,
or whether they may not have developed an
amount of latent virtue in the nation; whether
the convulsion has not heaved to the surface a
substratum of conscience and piety which has
hitherto been concealed under the rubbish of
filthy lucre and national corruption?

Doubtless both are, to an extent, true. Certain
results are of the war's creation, certain others
are of the war's development or modification.
And, indeed, I am disposed to lay some stress
upon the latter fact. It is most distinctly pointed
at in the great fact of to-day, that a whole nation
is before God with a song of praise upon its lips.
The custom in accordance with which we are
here this day, is no less a tradition than an act
called forth by the special issues of the time. It
carries us back to the fact to which I called your
attention on the last Thanksgiving occasion, that

2

the earliest civilization of New England, from which we have derived this custom, was essentially religious. New England itself was a mighty religious protest. Puritanism was a grand reaction; and, like all reactions from great abuses, was violent. As it swung back, it wrenched itself away from much that was lovely and of good report. Under its fierce impulse to denounce abuses, it often condemned, without discrimination, the things abused. I cannot admire nor sympathize with the early New England type of piety. Like its own granite hills, it was massive and majestic, storm-swept, and scarred by the avalanche. It lifted its sharp peaks above all the developments of its age; yet the snow lingered there, bidding defiance to the sunbeams. It afforded too little place for that liberal play of the softer affections; for those amenities, those tender sympathies, those graceful refinements, which would have softened its rugged outlines without impairing its strength or majesty. And yet for Puritanism, as first developed on New England soil, with all its errors, with all its repressive tendencies, with all its austerities, this nation may well return thanks to God. In its very absurdities there was a rude strength and dignity adapted to inspire something besides levity. If the channel in which it moved was

narrow, it was straight and deep; lying *through*
rocks and not round them. And as we have
come to see more and more clearly that the religious leaven of this land was destined to come
from New England, to see how vast was the
mass which it was destined to permeate, how
varied the characters and circumstances it was
ordained to affect, it has more and more appeared
what a fund of reserved power it was necessary
to have hoarded up there. If so many impressions must be taken from the religious development of New England, it was needful that the
lines of the original picture should be sharply
and deeply cut. If the block was to be wrought
by so many different chisels, and into such varied
shapes, it was needful that it should be hard.
The very excesses of New England Puritanism,
its almost morbid conscientiousness, its stringent
legalism, its insistence on doctrinal consistency,
its over-strained views of moral obligation, have
stamped it deep on the New England mind, and
through that have influenced the entire nation.
Its very rigidity, though relaxed by more liberal
views of mankind and of the Word of God,
has proved a partial safeguard, at least in New
England itself, against a violent reaction into
vice. The reaction has been, to a great extent, an intellectual one. The mind of later

generations has revolted from the gloomier dogmas of theology, and from over-stringent rules of duty. But the old training has left a mark on the New England conscience which cannot be easily erased. Even where men have abandoned its stern tenets for the more alluring realm of speculative philosophy, yet New England skepticism itself assumes the garb of religion, organizes churches, and proclaims the most startling heresies from pulpits; and enough of the old ground-work still remains to give to her that general aspect of order and thrift, that social stability and decorum which characterize no other portion of our land so decidedly. Puritanism may have made our New England fathers *stern* men, but it made them *upright* men. Loyalty to God, and the most absolute acknowledgment of his sovereignty, formed the very basis of their lives. Even patriotism would have been second to this sentiment, had it been possible for the two to become opposed in their path of duty. It made men of iron; but it was tempered iron that could hew for itself a way to Empire.

"They were men of present valor, stalwart old Iconoclasts,
Unconvinced by axe or gibbet, that all virtue was the Past's."

It made undemonstrative men, but it made thoughtful men. Though the tender, fireside emotions which so naturally seek expression, flowed far down in their hearts' secret places, yet the glimpse of them which would at times reveal itself, showed them flowing deep and strong, and pure as crystal; and though, at the domestic and social altars, Religion stood in the guise of a stern Vestal, pure as the snows of Katahdin, and as cold, never were those altars more sacredly guarded; never were their fires fed with sweeter incense; never was the sanctuary such a power; never were there exhibited richer fruits of filial reverence, fraternal affection, parental devotion, than in those early days. Never, in short, has religion so wrought itself into every department of life, civil, social and domestic.

Our present Thanksgiving is only one instance of the influence of New England religious institutions. Others might easily be cited, but it is matter of rejoicing that, with all the iniquity which has deluged us in the later years of our own national history, with all the lust for wealth which has hurried the people onward so madly, with all the national vanity and inflated self-importance which have blinded our eyes to the appreciation of more substantial elements of worth, the impulse both to proclaim and to celebrate a national acknowledgment to God still remains. Even though the proclamation were but a form, and the celebration naught but a merry-making, it is far better that even the form of a good institution remain, than that form and spirit should be alike extinct. For even the form, in its impaired beauty, may some day chance to call to men's remembrance a thought of its pristine loveliness, and lead them to seek some spell to revivify it.

But to-day's celebration is something besides a mere form. I question whether, for fifty years, there has been a public thanksgiving so nearly answering to the original spirit of the institution; marked by such a sincere outpouring of gratitude, and such a strong sense of indebtedness to God. This fact is too important to be overlooked in the consideration of our subject. For remember that it is a thanksgiving not only in the face, but in the midst of all the calamities and horrors and deprivations of war. Looking at the nation from a merely human stand-point, the causes for despondency and complaint might seem to over-balance those of thanksgiving. The war is at its height. Our hearts are sick with recitals of bloodshed. Our homes have been robbed; our firesides desolated; our communities have sent forth many of their bravest and best to return no more. Oh! how thickly the graves are crowded at Chattanooga and Atlanta, at Vicksburgh and Fair Oaks, at Antietam and Yorktown. From

the border-lines to the gulf the bones of Northern
youth lie bleaching; and desolated hearts, that
know not where their loved dead repose, go gro-
ping, with tears, in quest of every grave. The
weeds of widowhood have become a familiar
sight. The curse of Egypt is well-nigh repeated.
Scarce is there a house where there is not one
dead. The rebellion, too, while in many respects
its progress has been arrested, its strength deple-
ted, and its area narrowed, has, in some other
particulars, seemed to gain. It has infused a
larger share of its infernal venom into the hearts
of the free North. It has awakened fears of dis-
cord at home, that, for the time, have outweighed
the fear of defeat abroad. The emissaries of
rebellion have haunted our northern border, and
the chivalry have wrought their favorite deeds of
murder and pillage in our peaceful Northern villages, and have threatened our cities with flames
and robbery. Our enemy is yet defiant. We
have begun to feel the war at home. Its stern
necessities, and still more, the avarice and villainy
of those who regard it only as a means of filling
their pockets, have put the very necessities of life
out of the reach of many. And, to one looking
at these things as many do, walking by sight and
not by faith, thinking peace and prosperity the
highest of earthly goods. the present scene of

confusion, blood and death presents little occasion for gratitude. And seeing, as we do, so much of this purely worldly spirit, hearing men daily express their willingness to make any terms for peace, and talking of this and that thing having caused the catastrophe, as if it had not come round in the ordaining of a higher will than man's, it is at once surprising and gratifying, on sounding the general sentiment of the nation, to find it of an order so much higher, and tending to an especial degree of humble, heartfelt gratitude to God.

For this is no sudden, spasmodic development, called forth by a government proclamation, or by some temporary success of our arms. It is the expression of no shallow enthusiasm, momentarily gilded with piety. It is the flower of a longer growth — a growth in a hard soil, watered with tears, and tilled amid the rude shocks of war. The sentiment which breathes in our thanksgivings to-day; has found vent during the past year in frequent humiliation, in abject importunity at the throne of grace.

Earlier in the war we heard much talk of generals. When McClellan assumed the command of the army, you well remember how the popular favor bore him on the very crest of its wave, and how the popular mind would consent to entertain no thought but that of certain success, and abandoned itself to a delirium of hero worship. Under him organization was to be perfected. Under him the army was to be led to certain victory. Every heart accepted his words, " we have been beaten and have retreated for the last time," as an infallible prophecy. Oh! presumptuous nation thus to worship man and forget God! Oh! blind eyes! not to see that the purpose of God was not yet ripe. Oh! forgetful hearts! not to remember that the small grinding of the mills of God comes out of grinding slowly. And for this, our presumptuous folly and weakness, God did most fearfully rebuke us. It is not for me to say on whose shoulders rests the responsibility of that fearful Peninsular campaign, with its thousands of dead and fever-stricken victims. That is a matter of little moment now. But whoever was the agent, defeat and disaster were our lot, and God told us awful truths in the swamps of the Chickahominy, in the trenches of Yorktown, and in the crowded hospitals all over the North. God administered to us a fearful rebuke for the blasphemous folly of putting our trust in the arm of flesh. I think the nation took this and later lessons to heart, for I remember that when the tried hero who now commands our armies assumed his post — the man to whom the people's eyes had already begun to turn — his brow crowned with the freshest bays of victory, with every precedent adapted to inspire confidence in his skill and success, there was joined with the people's commendations of Gen. Grant's capacity and energy a deep and often expressed conviction that, without the interposition of a stronger arm, failure was to be his portion also. And you cannot have forgotten how, just ere that terrible Wilderness campaign, when every ear was on the stretch for tidings of battle, the people bowed their knees before God, and we, in those sultry afternoons, gathered ourselves together and poured out strong cries and tears to God for his aid in what we felt to be a dire extremity. What these prayers may have had to do with the achievement of what successes were gained, or in our deliverance from worse disaster than befel us, is not now the question. That they had their influence, and that a favorable one, I doubt no more than I doubt my own existence. Be this as it may, I thank God for the spirit which prompted to prayer. I thank God that the nation, whether through its immediate chastisement or through the reviving of the dying embers of conscience, showed itself so susceptible of discipline; that it was ready practically to repent of its folly, and acknowledge that its help came from God alone.

Nor is the more recent manifestation of the same fact to be forgotten. The recent election was one of the most peculiar crises that has ever occurred or could possibly occur in our history. We had demonstrated, as a government, our power of self-defence ; it remained for us to demonstrate our power of self-restraint. For you will remember that Democracy is now on trial ; the experiment of self-government is undergoing its crucial test. The test is only partial when government manifests sufficient energy and compactness to repel invasion. The more delicate question is, whether it may not fall in pieces by its own weight; and if it show .itself unpossessed of that restraining power which will keep it from anarchy within while engaged in war without, it proves itself not yet capable of self-government; unfit to be a force among the Empires. And, looking at this question antecedently, there was real reason to fear the test. It looked very much, at one time, as if the South had succeeded in securing the only weapon that would ensure her success — division at the North. For the questions which arose here, veil them as you might with party technicalities, resolved themselves into the simple alternative of loyalty to the Government of the United States, or compliance with the demands of the bogus government at Richmond.

They were thus questions adapted to call out the deepest feelings and strongest passions of men. The one party, willing to bear the burdens of war, and to make the sacrifices it demanded, bent only on conquering an honorable peace which should involve the entire and unconditional submission of the rebels, heard, with unfeigned horror, the proposal of another party to compromise when victory was within our very grasp. True, self-sacrificing patriotism, devotion to principles, stern determination to maintain the honor of the nation at any hazard, came into contact with devotion to party, devotion to men, self-interest, demagogueism, the spirit of compromise, and the love of slavery. I speak not as a partisan. Party lines were thrown down in this contest; and while I concede to many of the men whose political views differ from my own, purity of motive, and sincere conviction of duty, the line of division ran where I have just placed it. Loyalty or disloyalty was the issue. Patriotism on the one hand, and selfishness on the other, armed the hands of the North, and brought every power into the most vigorous action. The old, uncompromising New England spirit shook itself like a lion roused from his lair, and gathered itself for a decisive grapple with treason. The virus of the South, the spirit of her so called chivalry, which will rule or ruin, like a demon, had led the rabble captive at its will, and prepared them to insist on their demands by fair means or foul. Let secession journals and secession sympathisers sneer as they will, you know and they know that their threats were not empty. You know what traitors were plotting under the shadow of English neutrality. Let it be disguised as much as may be, the constitution and catalogue of the order of American Knights are on record to speak for themselves. The thousands of rifles and pistols secreted in Chicago, rise from their hiding-place and gleam a significant answer to denial. The tramping of horses through the peaceful streets of St. Albans, the crack of revolvers, the blood of unoffending citizens, and the public boasts of the miscreants, send down their challenge to contradiction and show what was in store for other cities of the North; while, blackest on the whole catalogue, branding the perpetrators with everlasting ignominy, stands that unparalleled meanness, that ineffable treachery which would have fastened a lie on our brave soldiers, living and dead, and made them the unconscious instruments of a party triumph. These were some of the forces at work in this struggle. Thank God, he did not abandon us. Thank God that official vigilance became His instrument for the exposure and overthrow of these diabolical plots. But looking at the state of things as it was, it had, I repeat, become a serious question how far the North would be able to exhibit the power of self-restraint, with the hands of a fierce and bloody war dragging at her skirts, and all these conflicting elements at their highest rage within. But oh! I, for one, am proud of my country. I praise God this day for my northern birth; and I call on you to join your gratitude with mine that we have lived to see the nation walk this fearful path with a quiet dignity, and consciousness of power, and a self-containment, which speak volumes for the influence of our earlier training and of our later discipline. Thank God, public virtue was not dead. Thank God that it had even grown to proportions that enabled it to take the barriers of party in the swing of its mighty stride, and to give no heed to them in its steady march for the right. Men abandoned party at this time who had never even split a ticket before. More men than ever before went to the polls asking themselves and God—" *What is right?*" and not—" *Who is the party candidate?*" More men interested themselves personally in the conflict than ever before. More men asked respecting the principles of candidates, and informed themselves accurately as to the issues pending, than ever before. And the national dignity and power that have asserted themselves at this crisis, and carried the nation triumphantly and peacefully through an exciting popular election in the midst of a civil war, will make themselves felt not only here, but far beyond the sea. They have been felt here already. They have manifested themselves in the subsidence of party bitterness; in the quiet acquiescence of the people's will; and they will be felt in the intriguing Court of France, and in the secret council chamber of her wily and ambitious head. They will be felt in perfidious England, with her ill-disguised hatred and her secret aid to rebellion. They will be felt and rejoiced in amid the snows of St. Petersburgh, and over the vast steppes of slave-redeemed Russia. They will be felt as forces in the tremendous revolution which is gathering its elements to re-model Europe; and the despot-trodden millions whose eyes have watched us through this shadow of death with straining eagerness, shall read in these manifestations new germs of hope for them and for the world.

But how happened it all? Oh! will any christian man ask me to believe that this sublime result, this ineffable good, was wrought out for us through human foresight or through military precautions? You may believe it if you can. I cannot. I ascribe this result, in great part, to prayer. In accounting for it, I find myself looking, not to the capitol at Washington; not to the head-quarters of Butler in New York; not to the arsenal across the river. I look into the secret places where men and women are prostrate before God. I see tears fall, and catch the sound of deep sighs and strong supplications. I look into the social gatherings for prayer in our churches throughout the North, and I find the nation a burden on all hearts; and, strange sound in such company, with the call to the polls, I hear mingled the call to prayer; I see altars of supplication smoking from east to west, and the incense of devotion, like a morning cloud, heralds the rising sun of the day of decision. Never did a war beget so much prayer. There have been bloody wars ere this, and thousands of prayers have winged their way heavenward on behalf of *individual* interests. Mothers and fathers have plead for their sons, and wives for their husbands, and friend for friend, asking for victory for a cause, but seeing, while they prayed, only him who represented the cause to their loving hearts. But while such supplications have ascended by millions from our stricken households, there has mingled with these individual sympathies and prayers a less selfish feeling that has risen into an amazing prominence. The nation has been a burden upon the nation's heart. Patriotism has separated itself, for the time, from the mass of individual hopes and sorrows, and has linked its arm with Religion's. And, out of the chorus of prayer, sounding deep and clear above its surging melody, like a church bell by the ocean, I hear lifting itself up the voice of a true patriotism; a patriotism instinct with the spirit of sacrifice; a patriotism intertwined with the deepest instincts of the nature; a love of country that corruption cannot sully nor disaster erase: and from such a patriotism, crowned with worship, no longer a sentiment but a force, constraining the nation to bend the neck of its pride, and to confess Christ as king, I draw larger hope than from the childish clamor of victory-bells, and music, and cannon, and the gay parade of waving banners.

It is a singular feature of the working of evil, that it continually produces its own alleviations. Its contact with good dashes out sparks which are the germs of cheering fires and friendly beacons. This feature has been exhibited in the present war, in its unprecedented development of christian activities and sympathies. The angel that has troubled the waters has imparted to them healing virtue. Private ministrations to the victims of war are of comparatively recent date. War has had to provide for its own victims,

4

When Florence Nightingale went through the Crimean hospitals, her lamp and very shadow hailed by the unfortunates that lay there as the harbingers of a guardian angel, the eyes of the world turned upon her with wonderment, and Europe, Asia, and America rang with her well deserved praises. But her fame and her reward are no longer unshared. Private ministration to the victims of war has become not only a familiar fact but an organized system, absorbing its millions of dollars, and enlisting its thousands of willing hearts and active hands. Where Scutari had one visitant, almost every battle-field, from Bull Run to the Shenandoah valley, has had its scores of ministrants, male and female. The Union army is not a band of mercenaries. It is a piece of the nation's life. Its elements are taken from beside our own hearthstones. They are not the refuse, but a large proportion of the youth and vigor, the wealth, intellect, and culture of our communities. Art and science have their representatives in the ranks, as well as bone and muscle; and not a camp or a vessel, or a battle-field is there but is linked, by many a tie, to peaceful homes in New England villages, or amid the farm-lands and cities of New York and Pennsylvania, or on the broad plains of the west. There was reason why the national heart should beat more quickly, and the national arm bestir itself more vigorously at the story of our soldiers' sufferings. And so, hand in hand with iron-mailed War, mingling its soft accents with the roll of the drum and the rattle of musketry, walked forth the holy Spirit of Charity, with hands laden with blessings, and sweet, sad eyes brimming with tears. Nor, because the national heart was thus touched, can it be truly said that these ministrations were, after all, selfish. They were more than relief sent from the family to its representative in the field. True, there never was a war in which home and the battle-field were so closely linked; but in each household, and in each community, the sufferings and dangers of their own representatives expanded instead of narrowing their sympathies; and the nation, for the time, merged itself into one great family, and set itself to provide alike for its thousands of children in the field. The same hallowed impulse that prompted that aged matron to kiss, for his mother, the cold brow of the unknown soldier, stirred the hearts and hands of thousands of mothers, wives and daughters throughout the land. Many a soldier on picket, in the bleak December midnight, has had occasion to bless the unknown hands to whom he was indebted for protection against the bitter cold. Many an one has thanked the unknown Sabbath-school child whose little fingers placed within his reach some of the simple conveniences of home, so sorely missed in the camp; and many a heart, amid the white tents and in the barracks and hospitals, will warm to-day at the remembrance of those whose thoughtful care and liberal hands have provided that the Thanksgiving feast at home should not be unshared in the field. Yet this has been but a part. On the field and in the hospital have been the sweetest, noblest manifestations of this grand national charity. Delicately reared ladies, who were wont to turn pale at a story of blood, walk fearlessly amid the sickening horrors of the battle-field, and the scarcely less sickening scenes of the hospital, binding up ghastly wounds, facing, without flinching, scenes that try the coolest surgeon, and offering to strangers the tender ministries of wives and mothers. Churches have given up their ministers; students have left their books; lawyers and merchants their offices, and joined the long march and shared the coarse fare of the soldier, and pillowed their unaccustomed heads beside him on the ground or on the floor. They have defied the pestilence and the bullet. They have shrunk from no hardship and from no exposure. They have yielded up life itself in this service. Passing through those rude, temporary hospitals, you may see them, now sitting by the sufferer, and penning for him the message of love to home which his wounded hand refuses to indite, now putting the cooling draught to his fevered lips, or reading to him the words of Christ, or binding up his wounds, or breathing a prayer into his dying ear. At the ambulance train, and on the transport with its groaning freight, they are to be seen moving to and fro, their hands full of supplies, and their lips teeming with the words of eternal life. Do you ask an explanation of this? It is religion thus brought into strange relation and contrast with war. The answer is best given in the words of a stranger at Belle Plain, where a few of us were at work on one of the transports. He stood upon the wharf watching us as we went from one to another, moistening the stiffened bandages, and bathing the fevered heads, until, at length, with his eyes filled with tears, and his lips quivering, he exclaimed, "How can you do that? How *can* you do it? Is it because you are christians?" Yes. Directly or indirectly these great organizations are the offspring of sentiments peculiarly christianity's own, and developed, in the order of God's providence, by the stern necessities of war. And as geologic convulsions sometimes throw gems to the surface, so this fearful earthquake of war has heaved into the light those two precious developments of christian charity, the Christian and Sanitary Commissions, which shall glow in the newly risen sun of peace among the most radiant of the nation's jewels of sacrificing love.

And, as in all similar cases, the charity has reacted upon its agents. While these efforts have diffused gladness throughout our armies, placed our sons and brothers in more direct communication with home, and alleviated the horrors of battle, they have played no small part in maintaining in the nation at large a tone of cheerfulness. Had mothers and sisters been compelled to sit with folded hands, and brood over the fearful possibilities of war, gloom and dismay would have settled like a pall over thousands of households. The awful suspense would have been too torturing for endurance. But the work of love for the absent soldier and for his comrades, all invested with a common interest through one, has kept many a heart from consuming itself, and enabled it to draw out of the very source of all its terrors, the elements of relief and hopefulness.

But there is still another aspect of this topic. God seems, in the agencies he has called into operation throughout the war, to have had an eye to the future, no less than to the exigencies of the hour. The reflex action of war is often as much dreaded as the war itself. War is a school of vice. The camp is generally the fountain-head of the worst corruptions; and when a million of the nation's youth and manhood go forth to serve for several years in that school, many of them disposed to the very evils most fostered by army life, and all of them susceptible of evil and exposed to temptation, it becomes a serious question what the result shall be when this mass shall have been re-absorbed into our population. Whether it shall come back upon us as a rushing tide of idleness, villainy and debauchery, or whether, by any possibility, these men shall return no worse than they went, and perhaps better. None can deny the reality and serious-ness of this danger. But to it is opposed one of the most extraordinary phases of war in any age or country. This is nothing less than a genuine, searching religious revival in the army. Time will not suffer me to go into details. The regular army chaplains, and especially the United States Christian Commission, have been God's chosen agents in this work; and through their vast machinery of publication, chapel-tents, tract dis-tribution, preaching the gospel, personal inter-course, and loving ministrations to both body and soul, a work is being done for Christ's kingdom, which bids fair to answer to a very considerable extent, the question, what kind of men our soldiers shall be returned to us. These agencies are growing so numerous, and so thoroughly and efficiently organized, that it is becoming difficult for the soldier to escape their action. Christian influence meets him as he comes fresh from home, and for the first time spreads his blanket amid the strange scenes of the "soldier's rest;" speaks to his homesick heart of a rest in heaven, warns him kindly of temptation, and points him to his only safeguard. It meets him in the person of the faithful chaplain, in the tent and at the camp-fire. It seeks him out as he lies stunned and bleeding on the field, and tells him the story of the cross, while it pours oil and wine into his wounds. It comes to his bedside in the hospital, and whispers words of peace, and puts into his hand the testament or the tract. Drunkenness, gambling, licentiousness have gone down before these efforts; and though much yet remains to be done, enough has been done to move the hearts of the church to a spontaneous outburst of praise. And I ask you to look at the philosophy of this movement and see, after all, how simple it is. The soldier, though exposed to temptation, is yet under circumstances peculiarly adapted to render him sensitive to religious impressions. His gayety is often assumed. He is

away from home, and the remembrance of its joys
and associations softens his heart. He is exposed
to death hourly; and few men can be entirely
careless in its presence. When sick or wounded
he craves sympathy. When near the dark valley
he gropes for a rod and staff to comfort him.
Now see how God has used this fact to make the
war, in one sense, a great evangelical movement.
Not only has he placed under such influences a
large class rendered more than usually susceptible by the training and associations of home, but
he has thrown within the sphere of the same
agencies a very large class that, in all human
probability, would have been reached by them
in no other way. I mean a class gathered from
the purlieus of our large cities; a class of pro-
fessional ruffians, not unfamiliar with the interior
of our jails, and whom no missionary efforts,
within my knowledge, have ever succeeded in
reaching. A host of such as these have thus been
massed, as it were, under the fire of the gospel,
amid influences peculiarly adapted to open their
hearts to its power. Thus God, in revealing himself as the Lord of War, has also stood revealed
as the Lord of Righteousness. Through all has
been manifest His inflexible will that even war
should forward the work of the Prince of Peace;
that out of its very privations and its constant

companionship with death should be evolved forces that should mould the rough soldier's heart anew, and send him back to his home a missionary of love and purity. The tide of war, as it rolls back, is not destined to deluge our cities and villages with vice and blasphemy. God has known the bane, and has furnished the antidote. And not only will the christian influences thus exerted *balance* the corruptions of war, but I venture to predict that they will turn the scale in their own favor; and history shall yet record, as the results of this conflict, the three great facts of an enslaved race set free, a people chastened into a higher national life, and an army in the field baptized with the power of the Spirit of God.

This Divine foresight does not cease here. There is another prominent exhibition of it in the elements of this conflict. This war is waged by a self-governing people. It must find its first impulse and its main-spring among the people. It is not for a king or an oligarchy to declare for war, and then call upon us to furnish its sinews. The people must be at once the moving and directing will, and the smiting arm. And the war's cessation will, therefore, send back into the great body politic a knowledge of war's horrors which must, in future, greatly predispose this nation to

peace. The scars will be upon the governing
power itself; and however great our future prosperity, however strong our temptations to ag-
gression, however adequate our ability to press
any claim which interest or caprice may prompt
us to prefer, we shall be likely, with the bitter
experience of these years of strife, to pause long
and to ponder well ere we commit ourselves again
to the tempestuous sea of battle. The war will
have cost us too much,—too many tears, too much
priceless blood, too many broken hearts. Its
lesson will have been branded too deep into our
national life and prosperity to make us anxious
to renew these scenes. And, as the kingdom of
Christ is to be a kingdom of peace, as we measure
its progress among nations, by this sign, among
many others, that diplomacy takes the place of
war, may it not be that, in this case, "the moun-
tains shall bring peace;" that in this turmoil
God is laying the foundations of a great calm ;
that even this war is the voice of one crying in
the wilderness, "Prepare ye the way of the Lord?"
Who shall say that our country, if she emerge
from this trial as now she bids fair to do, purified
and fitted to become an arbiter among the nations,
shall not, by her baptism of blood, be prepared
to throw her vast weight in favor of peace ? Who
shall say that she shall not only secure lasting

peace to herself, but be, under God, the instrument of a millenial reign to all the nations? Oh! it is a grand hope that the world shall yet behold her in all her gigantic proportions, radiant as the morning, though "scarred with tokens of old wars," with eyes benign, yet full of a light more terrible than the light of battle to her foes, throwing her sheathed sword into the scale and keeping it down, and with her voice of thunder crying Peace! Peace! to the fractious despots who, careless of blood, rave and clamor for war.

And America must henceforth occupy the position of an educator as well as of a peace-maker. This war is our punishment for many sins and wrongs, but, above all others, for the fearful wrong of slavery. Yet men have been slow to learn this, and in the midst of their sorest chastisement have been crying—"keep the negro out of the question;" "fight for the Constitution and the Union!" Ah! you *cannot* keep the negro out of the question. The Constitution was not broad enough to protect him at the first, and you cannot cover him with it now. He is woven into the question; and from the first he has resisted the attempt to cast him out of it. They tried to put him out of the question, and he came into the Union lines to start perplexing questions of law amid the hurry and tumult of preparation

for battle. They tried to put him out of the
question, and he came back again in the military
necessity which produced the emancipation proclamation. They tried to put them out of the
question, and they returned upon the secession
hosts in platoons and squadrons, with muskets in
their hands, and the fire of battle in their eyes.
They tried to kill them out of the question, by
denying them even the tender mercies of war,
and they came in the shape of demons, with
glaring eyeballs and fixed bayonets, replying to
every appeal of the prostrate chivalry, "*Remember
Fort Pillow!*" Yes! he is in the question, and he
is going to be in the question long after this war
shall have ceased. God has been teaching us by
our bereavements and by the horrible sufferings
of our brethren at the Libby and at Anderson-
ville; teaching the Union men of the South, by
their pillaged and burned houses, their aged
fathers murdered in cold blood, their outraged
wives and daughters; teaching all who have been
passive or lukewarm on the subject, the true
character of the spirit of slavery; implanting in
us the germs of a deeper sympathy with those on
whose poor heads has fallen the whole weight of
slavery's tyranny and lust and ignominy, and to
whom bereavement has been as necessary a part
of existence as labor. Nor does our work stop

with sympathizing. We have a debt, a fearful debt to the sons of oppression; and the so called Christian Civilization which has compromised so long with the sin, must now rouse itself to atone for the suffering. Africa turns upon us with its broken shackles in its hands, and, shaking them in our faces, demands that we show her the way to enjoy liberty. Her children came to us against their will, and now, whether *we* will or no, God commits them to our care. The question cannot be evaded. Their thousands are among us, they will be among us when the war shall have ended, and something must be done with them. They must be taught to labor. They must be taught to govern themselves. They must be led up out of the foul chambers of ignorance and brutality to which slavery has thrust them down. They must be christianized. Slavery has stood beneath the very shadow of the cross, and called its bleeding Victim to witness that its atrocities were all for Christ's sake, and, as a commentary upon its christian intentions, has compelled the slave to incorporate into his christianity the toleration of the foulest lusts; the denial of the marriage rite, the necessity of ignorance, the abrogation of all his rights as a father, or brother, or husband. Brutalized and degraded by such a christianity, he stands before the nation to-day, a pupil to tax the wisdom of the best skilled teacher; and it is for us, disciplined into sympathy with his woes by our own, shamed into a new appreciation of his rights and of our duties through the religious sentiment awakened by our chastisement, and made by the necessities of the war the arbiters of his destiny, to lead him again to the cross, and there refute the foul lie uttered by tyrants beneath its shadow, and read to him its lessons of love and protection and wisdom. For this God has spoken to the too lukewarm christianity of the North. For this, among other objects, he has been sifting, and testing and purifying it by suffering. And already we hear the response. Already the hum of study mingles with the rustle of the palmetto leaves and the murmur of the sea. Already the daughters and sons of the North have begun their mission, and sit enthroned in rude school-rooms, where the child of tender years and the child of gray hairs, bend together over the same page, and learn from their lips the rudiments of christian education. This work, so small as yet, but so well begun—begun in such a spirit of christian love and christian sacrifice, is only another of those points at which religion has developed its relation to war, and is a finger marshalling the nation along the way it must go, and pointing to its destiny as the educator and elevator of the race it has oppressed.

And now, if God has revealed himself in this conflict as the Lord both of war and of righteousness, if he has brought out of the desolations of war a quickened moral perception, a grand exhibition of christian charity, a spirit of humiliation and prayer, an impulse to evangelical effort; if, as we humbly believe, the nation is better fitted to-day than four years ago to be a representative of christian civilization, can we not see in all this indications of some new and larger results in the future? The question suggests itself whether we are to need a constant application of such discipline as has visited us for the past four years to keep us in the path, or whether we will receive our directions now in an humble and teachable spirit, and walk the remainder of our journey under gentler admonitions than war and desolation. Be assured, my brethren, the end for which God designs this nation, if we may presume to read his design in the obvious tendencies of his providence, is not our being the first military, or naval, or commercial power in the world; not our furnishing the grandest displays of intellectual vigor and power. All these the nation may attain; but they shall be, in the providence of God, but means to a higher, nobler end, her power as a CHRISTIAN CIVILIZATION. The "banner of the cross" is destined to wave side by side with the stars and stripes. Indications, I say, point to this. The facts of our origin point to it. Our Pilgrim fathers sought not "the wealth of the seas, or the spoils of war," but the shrine of a pure faith. American civilization has been, from the first, a standing protest against religious despotism. Democracy, in many essential particulars, and beyond any other form of government, is allied to christianity. If democracy could ever be pervaded, thoroughly, down to every individual, with the spirit of christianity, it would exhibit in human society that high ideal of christianity, the perfection of liberty with the perfection of restraint. Democracy developes the individual by the power of responsibility; and in this follows the example of christianity. Democracy is a mighty leveler; such is christianity. Democracy is full of the spirit of enterprise, and affords the largest room for its expansion. Christianity is the inspirer of all healthy enterprise. Democracy, appealing to conviction instead of prejudice, insists on the largest intelligence and culture. So does christianity. Democracy accommodates itself to the most varied forms of religious development, thereby exhibiting the same adaptation which marks christianity. In numerous respects

6

democracy reveals itself as the natural ally and agent of christianity. To all this we must add the fact, already adverted to, that God's purpose in the present state of affairs is a moral and not a political one. He has been teaching us that we were guilty, not unfortunate; that we were being punished, and not merely suffering from sore accident; that ghastly national sins and not errors of administration are at the foundation of our troubles; that we are to repent in sackcloth and· ashes, and not merely remodel political platforms and appoint new leaders. God has been striking, and trying to make us strike at elements unfavorable to the growth of a pure democracy; and these and other facts point to the conclusion that he is at work, preparing in this broad land a fit stage for the last act of the mighty drama, the consummation of human civilization. And for this the nation has had to undergo recasting. Base alloy had wrought itself into the fabric; the lust of money and of power, national idolatry and vanity, sensuality, brutality, and oppression of men for whom Christ died. I look back into the years past, and I see our own avarice, our own moral weakness, our complicity with sin, our overweening confidence and vanity and pride, heaping up fuel for the mighty fusion. I see secession, with the sneer of triumphant malice

on its lip, creep stealthily up from the marshes of
Carolina, and apply the torch. And to-day the
roar and glow of the furnace are at their fiercest.
To-day its lurid gleam tinges the snows that
watch the calm Pacific, and lights the bosom of
the Father of waters, and the lagoons of Florida,
and tips with fire the crests of the angry Atlantic.
Already the molten mass has begun to flow; a
fearful current, the blood of our sons, our bravest
and our best, our national hopes and aspirations,
our ambitions, our affections, our partisanships, our
pride, our strength, our prosperity, our political
theories, our national vanity, all pour fused together, through millions of gleaming musket
tubes, into the mould of our new life. I see not
the shape of that mould. Its delicate lines are
hid from mortal vision. But, while with you I
shrink from the hot blast of the furnace, while
with you I shrivel in its awful heat, through the
tremulously air I see one standing where the ham-
mers fall most quickly, where their dreadful beat
is loudest, where the lurid glow is reddest, where
the breath of the fire is hottest; and His form is
like unto the form of the Son of God, the Lord
of war and of righteousness. So long as my eyes
discern him there my heart shall not fear. So
long as I know that his potent rod is stretched
out over the fiery stream, I will bid it flow on,

though it leave blight and desolation in its track. For I know that when, at His word, the rude mould shall fall away, there shall rise from it a thing of beauty; a national life crowned as with the glory of noon-day; girt round with prayer, robed in purity, with love in its eyes and peace upon its lips, and in its hand the open charters of freedom and religion.

But, if we shall refuse to accept these indications,—if, following the beck of our national trial we press not on to that higher plane of national life where stands the altar of Jehovah, if we move not forward to higher virtue, to perfect freedom, better, far better, that some mountain billow had engulfed the Mayflower. Better that England had strangled our infancy in her cruel gripe. Better that we be even now put to flight before the armies of rebellion, and hunted from the land so unworthily occupied, until another, sterner, better race be led from some far off isle to accomplish the work of which we shall have proved ourselves unworthy.

" Freedom doth not consist
In musing with our faces toward the past,
While petty cares and crawling interests twist
Their spider threads around us, which, at last,
Grow strong as iron chains to cramp and bind
In formal narrowness, heart, soul and mind.

*   *   *   *   *   *